The 5 Day Momentum Method

Jeff Cooper

M. GORDON PUBLISHING GROUP
Los Angeles, California

Printed in the United States of America.

Published by M. Gordon Publishing Group, 1999.

ISBN 1-893756-03-3

Charts contained in this publication were created with SuperCharts® by Omega Research, Inc.

SuperCharts is a registered trademark of Omega Research, Inc.

Disclaimer

It should not be assumed that the methods, techniques, or indicators presented in this book will be profitable or that they will not result in losses. Past results are not necessarily indicative of future results. Examples in this book are for educational purposes only. These setups are not solicitations of any order to buy or sell. The author, the publisher, and all affiliates assume no responsibility for your trading results. There is a high degree of risk in trading.

Contents

Introduction

When I decided to write *Hit and Run Trading,* I knew there were a large number of people who were interested in very short-term trading (I define very short-term trading as a few hours to a few days). What amazed me (and my publisher) was just how big this world really is. We were so inundated with orders that the book had to go back for its fourth printing in eight months. What amazed me even more was the even larger universe of people who didn't day-trade but wanted a method that would allow them to trade while they went on with their everyday lives. These people did not want to (or cannot) sit in front of the screen all day (as I do) but they also didn't want to put up with the drawdowns associated with long-term buy-and-hold strategies.

In response to this need, the following is what I believe to be one of the best three- to seven-day trading methods available. This method, which is called *The 5 Day Momentum Method,* specifically identifies short-term pullbacks in strongly trending stocks and pinpoints where and when to enter to participate when the trend resumes.

THIS METHOD IS NOT THE HOLY GRAIL! It is, though, a very correct way to trade and it has proven itself over the years. More importantly, it applies to downtrending stocks as well as uptrending stocks which will allow you to profit no matter what type of market we are in.

Please read this course at least twice to make sure you fully understand the concepts and rules before trading. I also recommend paper-trading this method before using real money with it. This will allow you to better master the technique and increase the likelihood of your success.

Best of Luck with Your Trading!

Jeff Cooper

CHAPTER 1

The Method Behind
the Madness

One of the longest lasting and *truest* principles behind the nature of markets is this: strongly trending markets pullback for a few days and then resume their trend. This principle has been proven and exploited over and over. Recently, I wrote about it in *Hit and Run Trading* with the 1-2-3-4 strategies (three-day pullbacks), and Larry Connors and Linda Raschke wrote about it in their book *Street Smarts* where they illustrate that strongly trending markets tend to pullback to their 20-day moving average before rising again. If you go through the body of trading literature on a historical basis you can find reference to this concept and as far back as the early 1900s, when W.D. Gann wrote about it.

What happens is that a strongly trending (runaway) market will take a few days rest before continuing its trend. This is especially true in the early stages of the move. The rest, or pause, will come in the form of sideways movement or a few down days (up days for downtrending markets). This comes mostly from individuals who were lucky enough (or smart enough) to have bought at lower levels (or, in downtrends, who had shorted at higher levels) and now wish to lock in their gains. However, this pullback, or rest, is also used by the momentum growth funds and traders as a way to accumulate more stock at lower levels (or, on the downside, unload stock at higher levels), therefore once again causing prices to move higher and creating more momentum. How far these stocks run is absolutely impossible to predict but the key is to climb aboard early and let the market go where it will go.

If you go back 100 years and look at stock prices (and in fact commodity prices), you will see this scenario play itself over and over and over. The age-old question is, where do you enter the market to provide you with the highest possibility of profit while taking the lowest degree of risk? I believe The *5 Day Momentum Method* does the best, most efficient job of answering this question. *The 5 Day Momentum Method* identifies *only* the *strongest* trending stocks and, with the use of an oscillator, pinpoints when the pullback will likely exhaust itself and the trend will resume.

Let's now move on to the mechanics and calculations needed to use this methodology.

CHAPTER 2

ADX and Stochastic Indicators

The *5 Day Momentum Method* utilizes two indicators to identify the correct entry-point. The first identifies the trend and the second identifies the pullback. In my opinion, ADX measures the trend better than any other method (we will discuss Relative Strength in a moment). For those of you who are new, ADX stands for Average Directional Movement. The ADX measures the *strength* (not direction) of the trend. **The higher the ADX reading, the stronger the trend.** The *5 Day Momentum Method* only trades stocks whose ADX reading is 35 or higher. This means we are only looking at stocks that are moving *strongly* in one direction. To identify the direction, we use the ADX companion +DI and –DI. Simply, if the trend is up, the +DI will be greater than the –DI and if the trend is down, the –DI will be greater than the +DI. (If you are a bit confused, the examples will simplify this for you).

Therefore, if we are looking to buy into a strongly trending stock, its ADX reading must be 35 or higher (the calculation for ADX is in the appendix) and its +DI reading must be higher than its –DI reading. If we are looking to short a downtrending stock, the ADX reading must be 35 or higher and the –DI reading must be greater than the +DI reading.

ADX requires you to have a software program to do its calculations. Several software programs provide this (a partial list is in the appendix) but if you cannot obtain this calculation, the next best choice of indicator to use is Relative Strength (RS) used by Investors Business Daily. The RS readings identify how a stock has performed over the past 12 months versus other stocks. A reading of 99 means that the stock has outperformed 99 percent of all other stocks. Ideally, you want to only buy stocks with this method that have a RS reading of 95 or higher. This assures you of being in the strongest uptrending stocks available. On the short side though, RS does not amply identify the tradable downtrending stocks. A very low RS reading (1-10) is usually associated with very low-priced, nearly bankrupt stocks. Also, we do not want to trade very low priced stocks due to their lack of movement and therefore low RS is virtually useless for shorting purposes. One solution I may suggest is to look at the Falling Relative Strength List that Investors Business Daily provides of stocks recently trading *under* the RS 50 level and RS 30 level. These are stocks that are certainly sinking and they make good candidates to include in the short-selling universe.

The second indicator to complete our toolbox is stochastics. Stochastics are a mathematical formula (see appendix) that is based on the fact that as prices increase, closing prices tend to be closer to the upper end of the price range, and as prices drop, their close is usually near the bottom of the daily range. Conventional wisdom states that when readings get under 40 percent the market is oversold and above 60 percent the market is overbought. There are four components of stochastics—Fast % K, Fast % D, Slow % K, and Slow % D. **The only one we need to concern ourselves with is Fast % K.** This is an *extremely* sensitive component, and it allows us to best measure overbought and oversold conditions. (A sidenote needs to be added—I have read and studied many books that attempt to teach people how to trade using stochastics and for the most part they are useless. The reason is that in strongly trending upmarkets, these oscillators will tell you the market is overbought, but unfortunately markets can remain this way for days and weeks. The reverse is true for downtrending markets. Traders get killed selling into these markets as they continue to rise.)

If all this sounds complicated, it really is not. Once we look at the examples, the pieces will be easier to understand.

For *The 5 Day Momentum Method* we use an *eight period Fast % K* for our calculations. In uptrending markets, we want the Fast % K to drop to *40 percent or under.* This means the market has pulled back (oversold) and there is a higher than average likelihood the market will again move higher. In downtrending markets, we want the Fast K % to climb to *60 percent or higher.* This means the market is overbought and the down-trend is likely to kick in again.

Again, if this is a bit difficult to understand, please be patient. I promise you that within 60 minutes it will be second nature to you.

CHAPTER 3

Putting Everything Together

Let's review the rules from the previous section and add the final pieces:

1. We will only trade in THE STRONGEST TRENDING STOCKS. This means we will only buy stocks whose ADX is 35 or higher and whose +DI is greater than its −DI reading. If we do not want to use ADX, we will use Investors Business Daily Relative Strength Reading and only trade stocks whose Relative Strength reading is at 95 or higher.

    For downtrending stocks (short selling), the ADX must be 35 or higher and the −DI reading will be above the +DI reading. If we use RS, we want to short those stocks who have recently dropped to under 50 or 30 as mentioned in Investors Business Daily.

2. **Price is critical!** The higher the price, the better. Testing has shown that stocks priced above 50 perform better using this method than stocks priced above 40 and stocks priced above 60 perform better

than stocks priced above 50 and so on. Unfortunately, as we move into the higher price range we have fewer and fewer situations to choose from. *Therefore, we will only trade stocks on the long-side whose price is above $50/share.*

For short sales, we will drop the requirement to above $40/share. This is because stocks drop quicker and their daily range is larger to the downside.

3. When we have limited our trading universe to rules 1 and 2, we will wait for a Fast % K stochastic setup.

For Buys:

A. Today (Day One), the Fast % K must close under 40 percent. This tells us we are oversold.

B. We will buy tomorrow (Day Two), one tick above today's high (1/16 point). If you are not filled tomorrow (Day Two) you will look to buy the next day (Day Three, a tick above the Day Two high). We allow ourselves two days to get in after each under 40 reading to allow for one day consolidations that push the Fast % K above 40 (again, the examples will clarify this further).

C. Upon being filled, our stop is at or 1 tick under the previous day's low. This means if today's range is 54 for the high and 52 for the low, we will buy tomorrow one tick above 54 and our stop will be at 52 or 51 15/16. Unless the market does something crazy overnight, this will be our maximum risk on the trade.

For Short Sales:

A. Today (Day One), the Fast % K must close above 60 percent. This tells us we are overbought.

B. We will sell short tomorrow (Day Two), one tick below today's low (1/16 point). If you are not filled tomorrow (Day Two) you will look to sell the next day (Day Three, a tick below the Day Two low). We allow ourselves two days to get in after each above 60 reading to allow for one day consolidations that push the Fast % K below 60 (again, the examples will clarify this further).

C. Upon being filled, our stop is at or 1 tick above the previous day's high. This means if today's range is 66 for the high and 63 for the low, we will sell short tomorrow one tick below 63 and our stop will be at 66 or 66 1/16. Unless the market does something crazy overnight, this will be our maximum risk on the trade.

Let's look at a handful of examples on how to enter a trade.

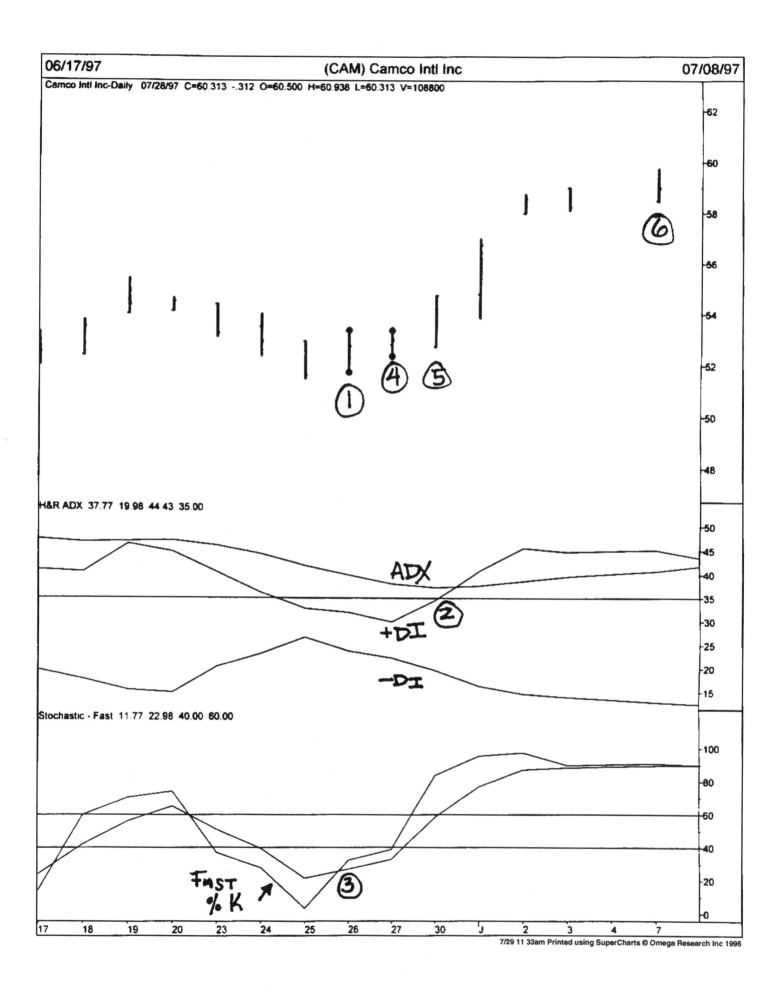

Camco Intl Inc-Daily   07/28/97   C=60.313   -.312   O=60.500   H=60.938   L=60.313   V=108800

H&R ADX   37.77   19.98   44.43   35.00

ADX

+DI

-DI

Stochastic - Fast   11.77   22.98   40.00   60.00

FAST % K

7/29 11 33am Printed using SuperCharts © Omega Research Inc 1996

Camco

1. Camco is trading above $50/share.

2. The ADX is above 35 and the +DI is greater than the –DI.

3. The Fast % K stochastic reading is under 40. (We ignore the Fast % D which is the other line).

4. We place a buy stop one tick above the previous day's high and we do not get filled. We will try again tomorrow. (Remember: Even if the stochastic reading goes above 40, you try one more day).

5. We get filled and our protective stop is near yesterday's low.

6. A 10 percent move in a week.

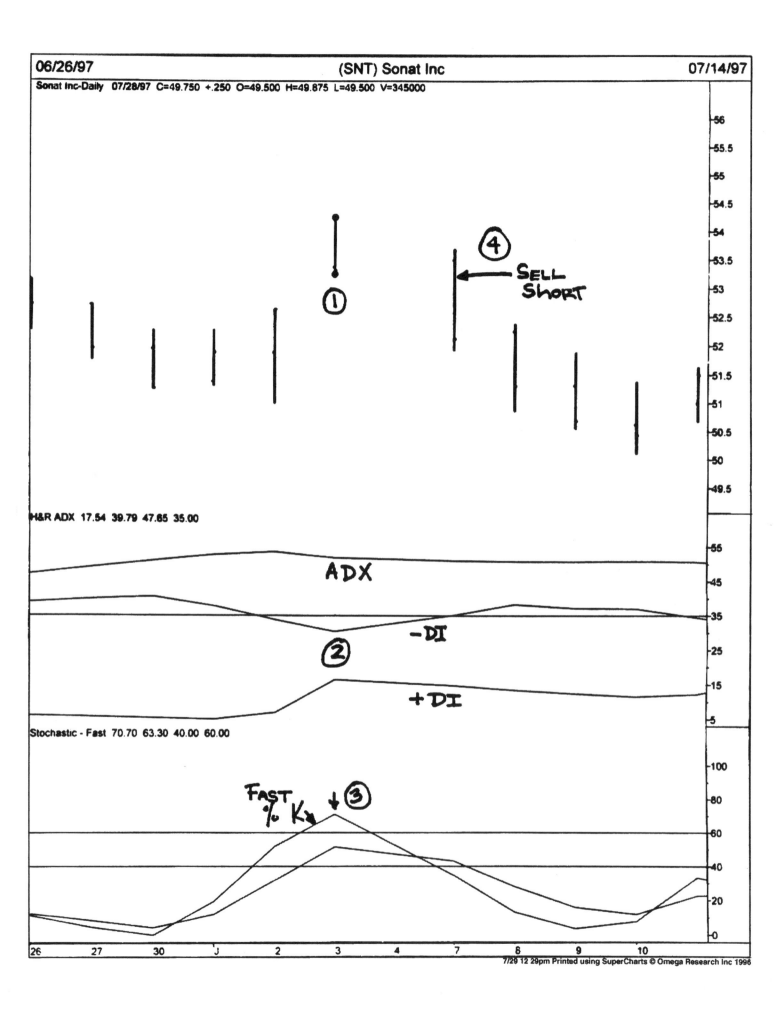

Sonat

Here is a short sale.

1.   The stock is trading above $40/share.

2.   The ADX reading is well above 35 and the trend is down because the –DI is greater than the +DI.

3.   The Fast % K stochastic moves above 60 signifying a signal.

4.   We sell short at 53 3/16, one tick under the previous day's low. Our stop is near yesterday's high.

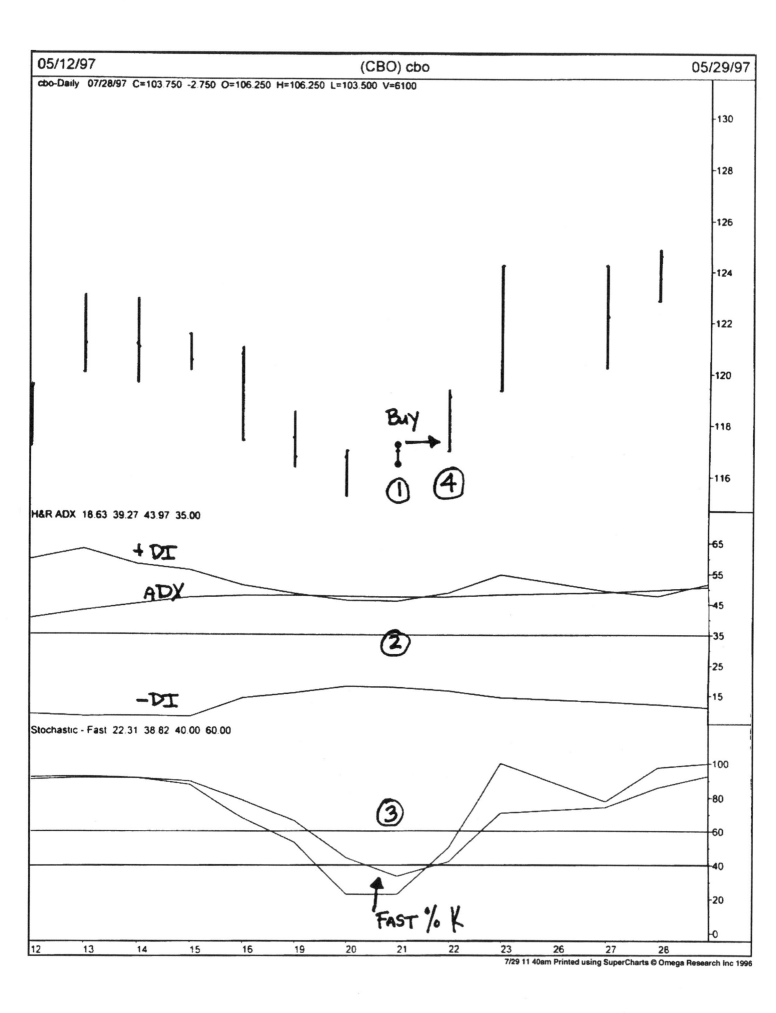

CBO

1. The stock is priced over $50/share.

2. The ADX reading is above 35 and the +DI is greater that the –DI signifying the trend is up.

3. The Fast % K reading is under 40 (we ignore the Fast % D which is the other line) telling us a pullback has occurred.

4. We buy one tick above the signal day high at 117 1/2 and our protective stop is near the previous day's low.

Please notice the stochastic reading was above 40 on May 20, therefore a signal wasn't triggered.

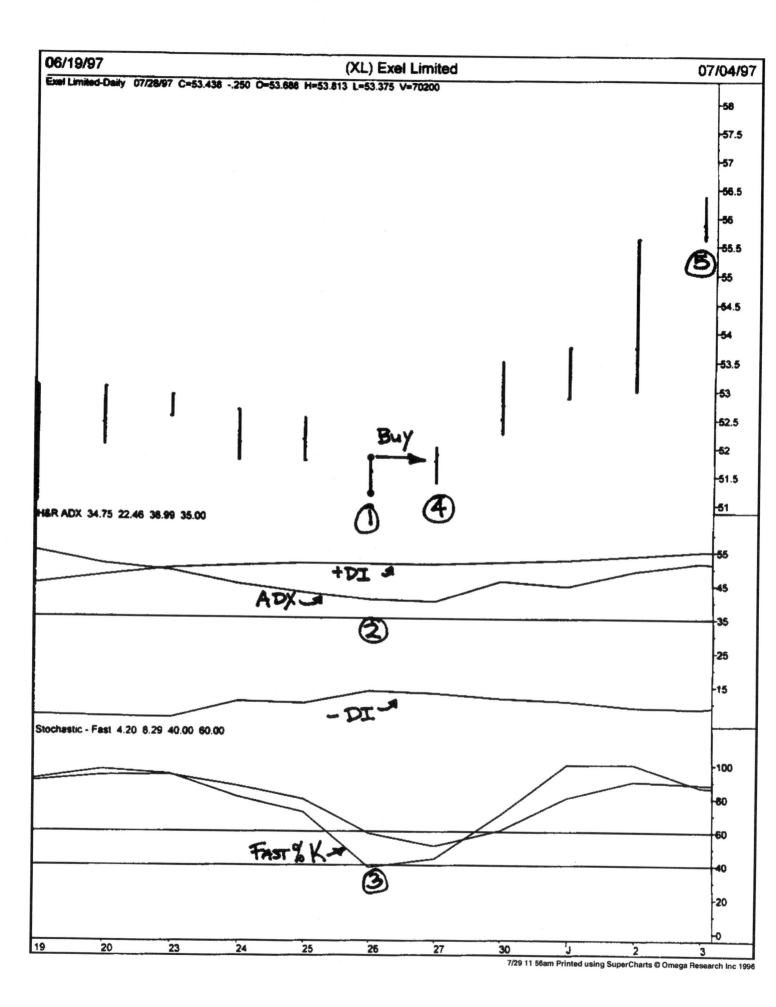

Exel Limited

1. The stock is trading above $50.

2. The ADX reading is above 35 and the +DI reading is greater than the –DI reading. This tells us the trend is up.

3. The Fast % K drops under 40.

4. Buy one tick above yesterday's high of 51 13/16. Our protective stop is near the previous day's low.

5. Exel moves more than 4 points higher.

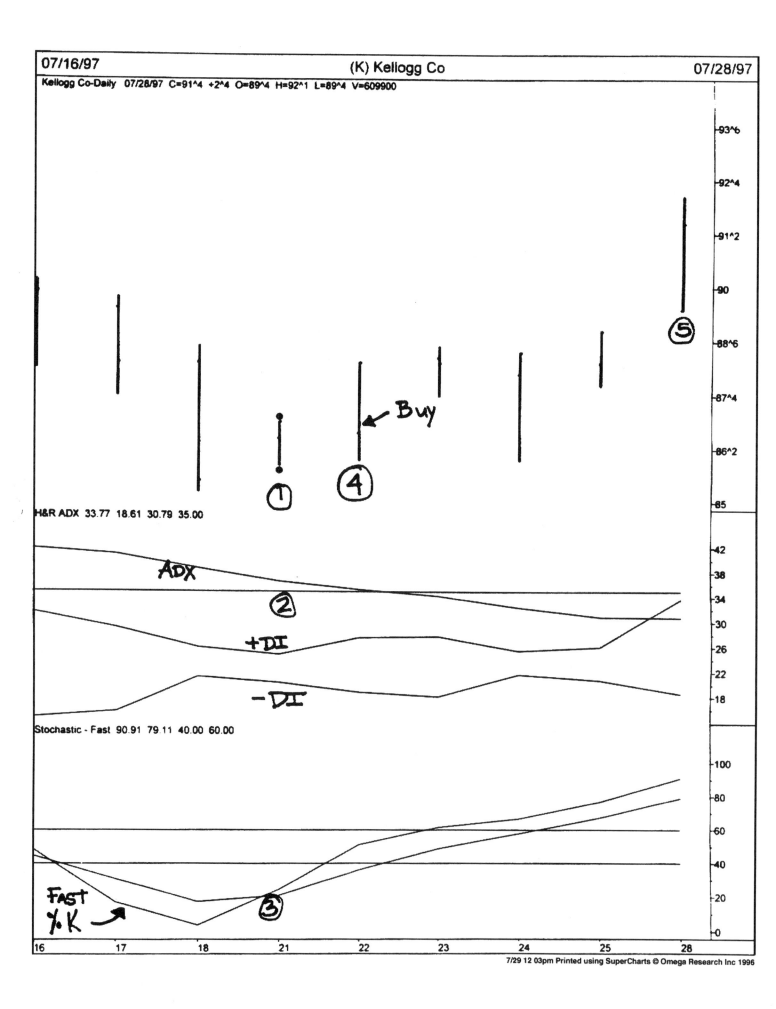

Kellogg

1. Here is a solid move from a fairly conservative stock. Kellogg is trading above $50.

2. The ADX is above 35 and the +DI is greater than the –DI.

3. Fast % K is below 40.

4. Buy at 86 7/8 and our protective stop is near 85 13/16. Our risk is approximately 1 1/16 points.

5. The stock moves nearly 5 points in 5 days.

CHAPTER 4

When to Get Out

Earlier, I mentioned that *The 5 Day Momentum Method* was an ideal strategy for traders who did not wish to or could not sit in front of a trading terminal all day. Because the strategy is a one- to seven-day setup, you can place the entry stops with your broker and give instructions for the initial protective stop upon being filled. From there, you have two exit choices. The first is simply a five-trading-day exit and is specifically for those individuals who are just too busy to be more proactive. The second exit strategy is a more dynamic strategy and allows you to maximize gains further.

The 5 Day Exit

Research on *The 5 Day Momentum Method* has found that the average period to maximize gains after being filled is five trading days (hence, the name). This gives the trade enough time to develop as the trend kicks back in. Therefore the exit rules are as follows:

1. Upon being filled, place a protective stop near the low of the previous day's bar (near the high of the previous day's bar for short sales). This should be a good til canceled (GTC) order and it will remain intact until you are filled or you have canceled the order.

2. If you are not stopped out, exit the trade on the close four trading days from today. This means if you are filled on Monday, you will exit on Friday (this keeps you in the position for five trading days, Monday inclusive).

This is the simplest way to trade. You are simply exiting the trade upon either being stopped out or five days later, which is likely a profit. Please remember to cancel your good til canceled stop order upon being filled on the fifth day. Failure to do this can be not only embarrassing, but also quite costly.

Finally, the one suggestion I may add to this comes when you have an extraordinary gain. It is quite frustrating to allow a large profit to vaporize because you are waiting for the fifth day. Therefore, on profits you are happy with, sell half your position (and cancel half your GTC order) and let the other half go the full period. This should basically give you a very solid chance of furthering your overall gains.

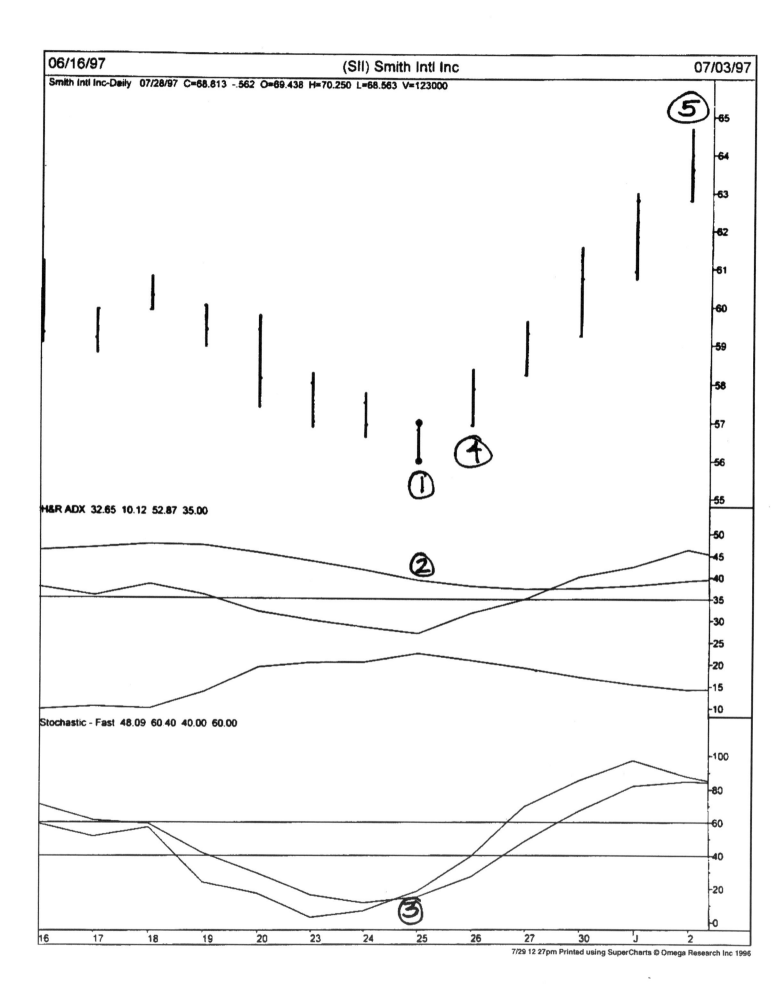

Smith Intl Inc-Daily 07/28/97 C=68.813 -.562 O=69.438 H=70.250 L=68.563 V=123000

H&R ADX 32.65 10.12 52.87 35.00

Stochastic - Fast 48.09 60.40 40.00 60.00

5 Day Exit

SII

1. Smith International is trading above 50, off its pullback.

2. The ADX and +DI, −DI signify a strong uptrend.

3. The Fast % K stochastic is under 40.

4. We buy the next day at 57 1/16. Our protective stop is at 56.

5. Five days later, we exit at 63 5/8 and we cancel our stop. Our reward/risk was 7-1.

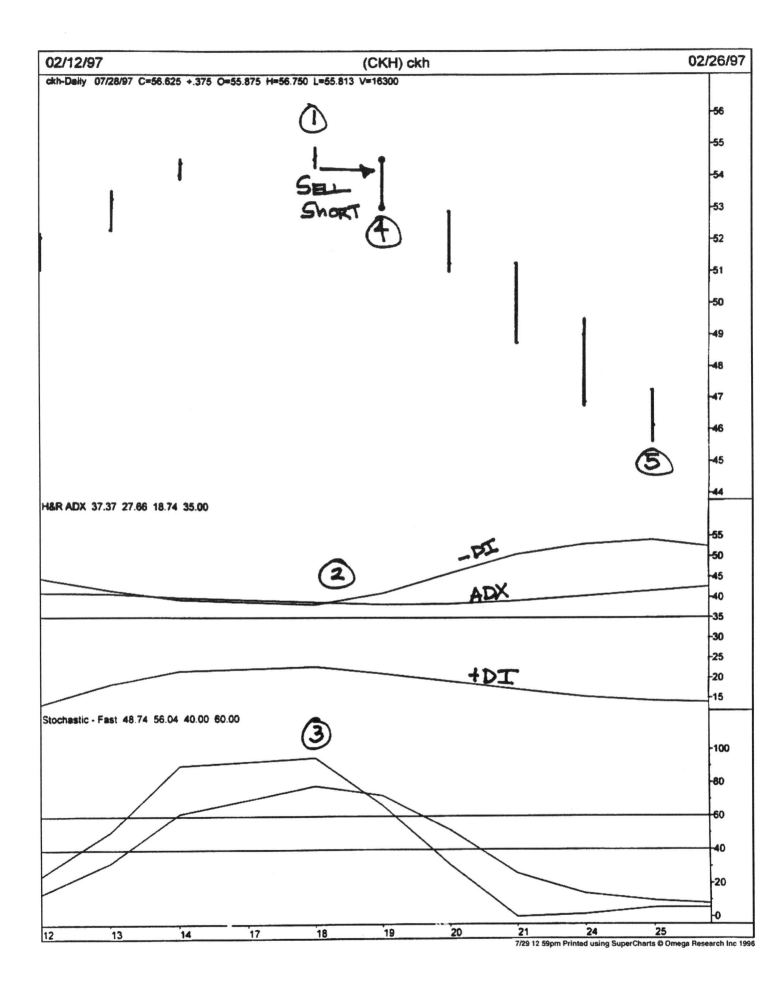

ckh-Daily 07/28/97 C=56.625 +.375 O=55.875 H=56.750 L=55.813 V=16300

SELL
SHORT

H&R ADX 37.37 27.66 18.74 35.00

-DI

ADX

+DI

Stochastic - Fast 48.74 56.04 40.00 60.00

CKH

1.   The stock is above $40/share.

2.   ADX signifies a strong downtrend.

3.   Stochastic above 60.

4.   Sell short at 54 1/8, one tick under the previous day's low and place a stop near the previous day's high. Remember, the protective stop should be placed, Good Til Canceled (GTC).

5.   We buy back our short position 8 points lower and cancel our stop order.

The Trailing Stop Exit

This exit strategy requires you to be more hands on and the added effort should increase your profits by an added amount.

Here is how to execute the exit strategy:

For Buys:

1. Upon being filled, place your stop at or near the bottom of the previous day's bar.

2. Measure the risk of your trade and upon profiting by that much move your stop to break-even. This means if you buy at 52 and your initial protective stop is at 50, your risk is 2 points (commissions are omitted). When the stock trades up to 54 (2 points) your protective stop immediately moves up two points to 52 and puts you in the position of, at worst, scratching the trade (barring an unforeseen calamity).

3. When the stock moves to a price that is double your initial risk, sell half. This means at 56 (double the initial 2 points risk) you will take profits on half the position.

4.   Let the other half run as you see fit. It is impossible to know how far the trend will carry the position and, by trailing the stop, you have the chance to further maximize your gains.

For Short Sales:

1.   Upon being filled, place your stop at or near the top of the previous day's bar.

2.   Measure the risk of your trade, and upon profiting by that much, move your stop to break-even. This means if you sell short at 59 and your initial protective stop is at 61, your risk is 2 points (commissions are omitted). When the stock trades down to 57 (2 points) your protective stop immediately moves down two points to 59 and puts you in the position of, at worst, scratching the trade (barring an unforeseen calamity).

3.   When the stock moves to a price that is double your initial risk, buy back half. This means at 55 (double the initial 2-point risk) you will take profits on half the position.

4.   Let the other half run as you see fit. It is impossible to know how far the trend will carry the position and by trailing the stop, you have the chance to further maximize your gains.

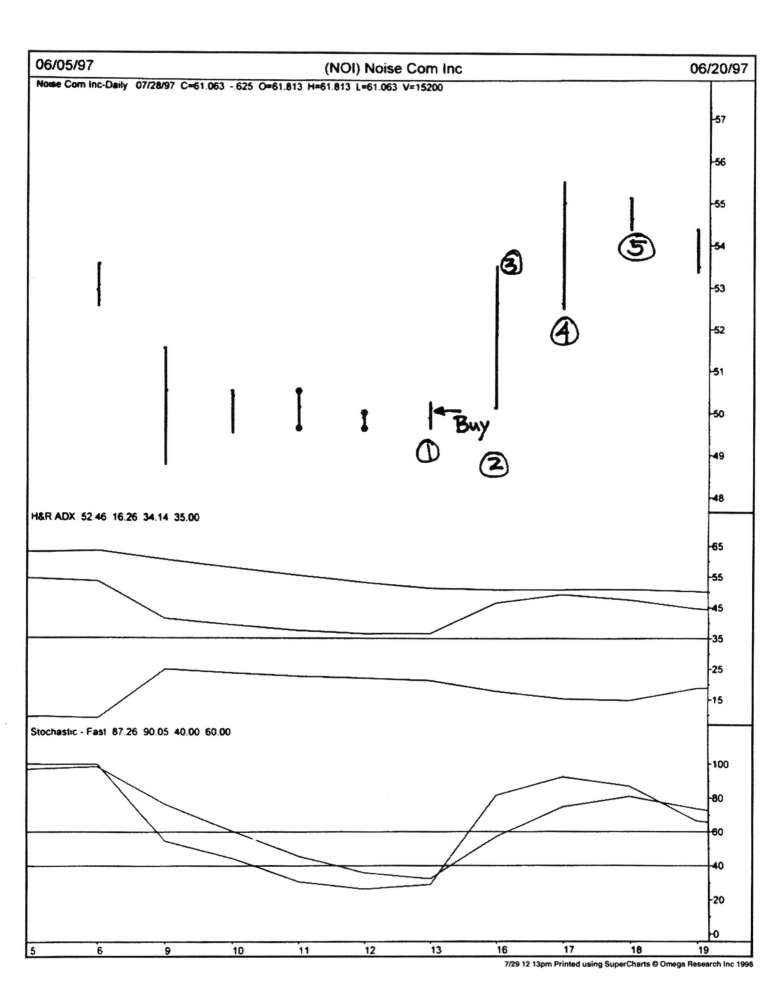

Noise Com Inc-Daily 07/28/97 C=61.063 -.625 O=61.813 H=61.813 L=61.063 V=15200

H&R ADX 52.46 16.26 34.14 35.00

Stochastic - Fast 87.26 90.05 40.00 60.00

Buy

7/29 12 13pm Printed using SuperCharts © Omega Research Inc 1996

NOI

1. We enter NOI at 50 1/8 and our stop is at 49 3/8 risking 3/4 points (not including slippage and commissions).

2. The next day the stock rises intraday to 50 7/8 which is equal to our initial risk. We therefore raise our stop to yesterday's entry of 50 1/8.

3. The stock continues to rise and we have doubled our return versus our risk and we take profits on half the position.

4. The stock remains strong and we raise our stop by at least one point or more to lock in further profits.

5. The stock closes under where it opened and we should strongly consider exiting, as it appears the momentum has faded.

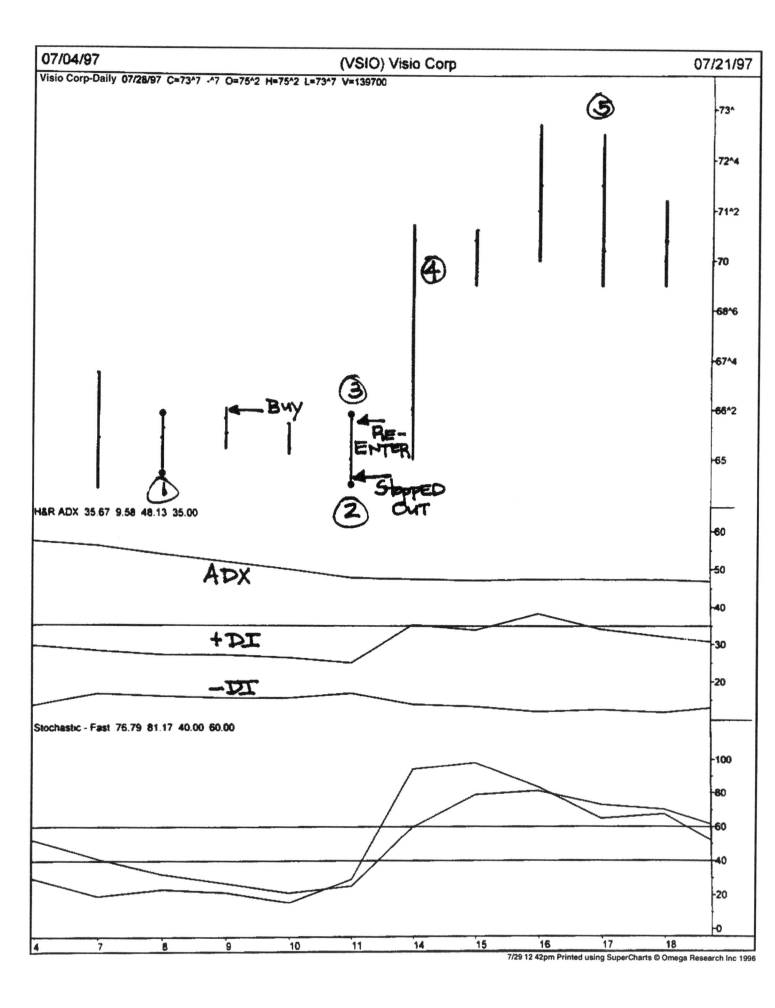

Visio Corp

1. A setup and we are filled the next day.

2. Two days later, we are stopped out for a loss. Please notice though we again intraday have a signal.

3. We enter at 66 and our stop is at 65 1/4 risking 3/4 of a point.

4. Intraday, our position moves equal to our initial risk and we move the stop to breakeven. When the stock rises to 67 1/2 (double our risk), we take profits on half.

5. As the stock rises, we will trail our stop higher to lock in the remaining profits.

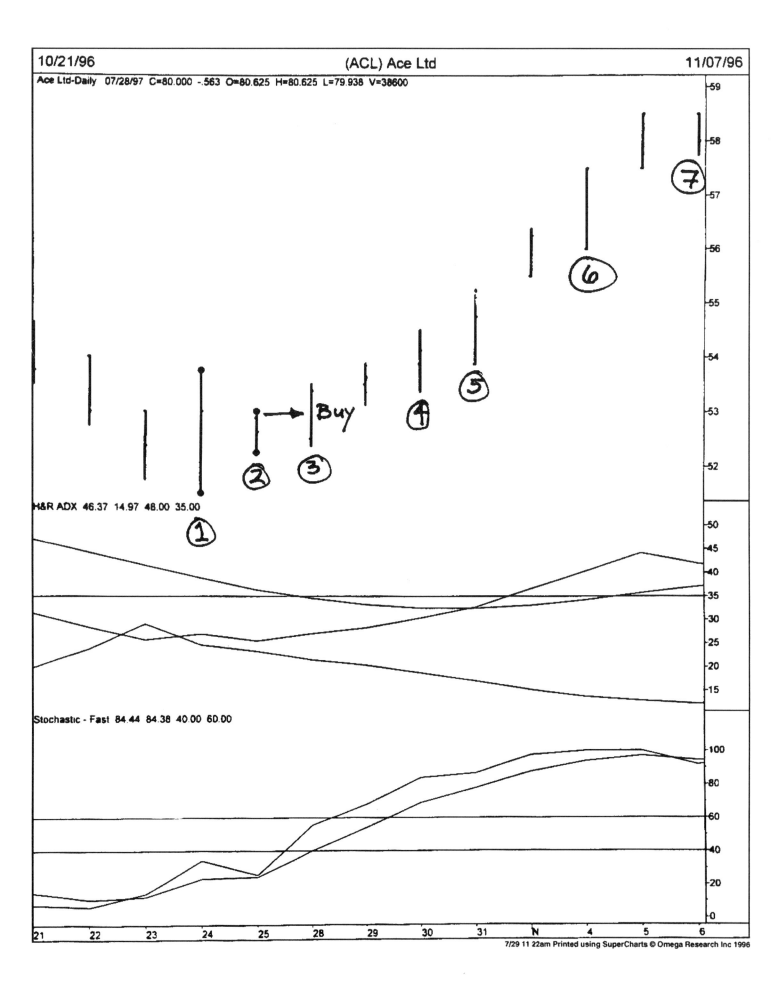

Ace Ltd-Daily   07/28/97   C=80.000   -.563   O=80.625   H=80.625   L=79.938   V=38600

H&R ADX   46.37   14.97   48.00   35.00

Stochastic - Fast   84.44   84.38   40.00   60.00

Ace Ltd.

1.   A buy signal.

2.   No entry, as we do not trade above the previous day's high.

3.   We enter at 53 1/8 and our initial protective stop is at 52 1/8 risking 1 point.

4.   The stock rises 1 point (our initial risk) and we move our stop to breakeven.

5.   At 55 1/8 (double our risk), we sell half.

6.   As the stock rises, you should raise your stops to protect your profits.

7.   A down day—profits should be locked into near the $58 range.

In conclusion, exit strategies are always a bit more difficult than entry strategies. I realize the trailing stop exit is more complicated than the five-day exit, but if you have the time and ability to utilize it, your returns should be greater.

One final note to remember: you are risking a fairly small amount (usually a few points) in order to make larger gains. Therefore it is critical to adhere to the protective stop rules. Small losses can be survived but large losses will definitely kill you. This can be avoided with good discipline on your part.

CHAPTER 5

Money Management

We have discussed the importance of stops and I would like to again mention it. I know of too many traders who allow one loss to wipeout many gains. *The 5 Day Momentum Method* is a fairly low-risk (compared to other trading systems I have come across) trading strategy that hits lots of singles. **PLEASE NOTE:** In backtesting the method on a universe of over 500 stocks (above $50/share) over a seven year period, there was an approximately 1 5/8 point average gain per trade over a five day period. The method was successful a little *under 50 percent of the time* (due to being stopped out). This means that the profit to loss per trade was approximately three to one. Some trades had home-runs, and the remaining winning trades grinded out small gains. **Therefore, allowing a loss to run on you will greatly lower your chances for success.**

On the percentage returned side, the results are excellent. If we lower our 1 5/8 point average trading profit by 3/8 point for the spread and slippage (this is generous) and another 1/8 for round-trip commission (6 cents per share), we still are left with 1 1/8 points per trade. The average price of the stocks tested was approximately $71 per share. Therefore, each trade made 1.58 percent for five days work! (1 1/8 divided by 71)

Annualize this on a one trade per week basis and the results are staggering. Is this return guaranteed? *Absolutely Not.* It only shows that on a historical basis, **The 5 Day Momentum Method** provided a healthy edge to those willing to follow the rules and use proper money management.

I cannot stress strong enough the importance of remembering this when the urge to ignore your protective stops arise. It is the single most common reason why traders fail, and if you wish to avoid joining their club, protect yourself and abide by the rules!

CHAPTER 6

Trading Options with *The 5 Day Momentum Method*

I will begin this section by telling you I am not an options trader. I trade equities and this keeps me busy enough. There are, though, many people who focus on the options markets as a leveraged way to make their money grow. Unfortunately, the overwhelming majority of traders lose money buying options. My observation is they commit two trading sins: 1) They *guess* where the market (stock) is going and 2) when they are wrong, they don't use stops and they let their options go to zero. In my opinion, *The 5 Day Momentum Method* lends itself well to short-term options trading and it helps cleanse the above mistakes.

In order to utilize *The 5 Day Momentum Method* with options, you need to *apply the exact same rules* you would use as if you were trading the underlying equities. The only difference will be is that you will be buying deep in the money calls for long setups and deep in the money puts for short setups. Also, you will purchase the options only after the signal is triggered on the underlying equity. This means that if *The 5 Day Momentum Method* buy stop is to be triggered on the stock at 57 3/4, you will not buy the options until the stock trades at that price.

Now the question to answer is, which options to trade? You should be at least 2 strike prices in-the-money to minimize the option premium. In the above example, we used 57 3/4 as the trigger price. Therefore the 55 calls are one strike in the money and the 50 calls are two strikes in the money. The front month 50 calls are the ones to focus on and to buy (if the expiration date is within 5 trading days, trade the following month options). As far as exit strategies, they are identical to the equities. Protective stops should be in place at the same levels as the stocks and you should exit in the same manner.

One last point should be made. As I mentioned earlier, the higher the price of the stock you are trading, the larger the profit. Therefore, it is even better to focus on the options whose underlying stock price is above 80 or 90 or higher. Again, the higher the stock price, the better!

Let's look at a few examples to help further understand the above:

SEE OTHER SIDE FOR CHART.

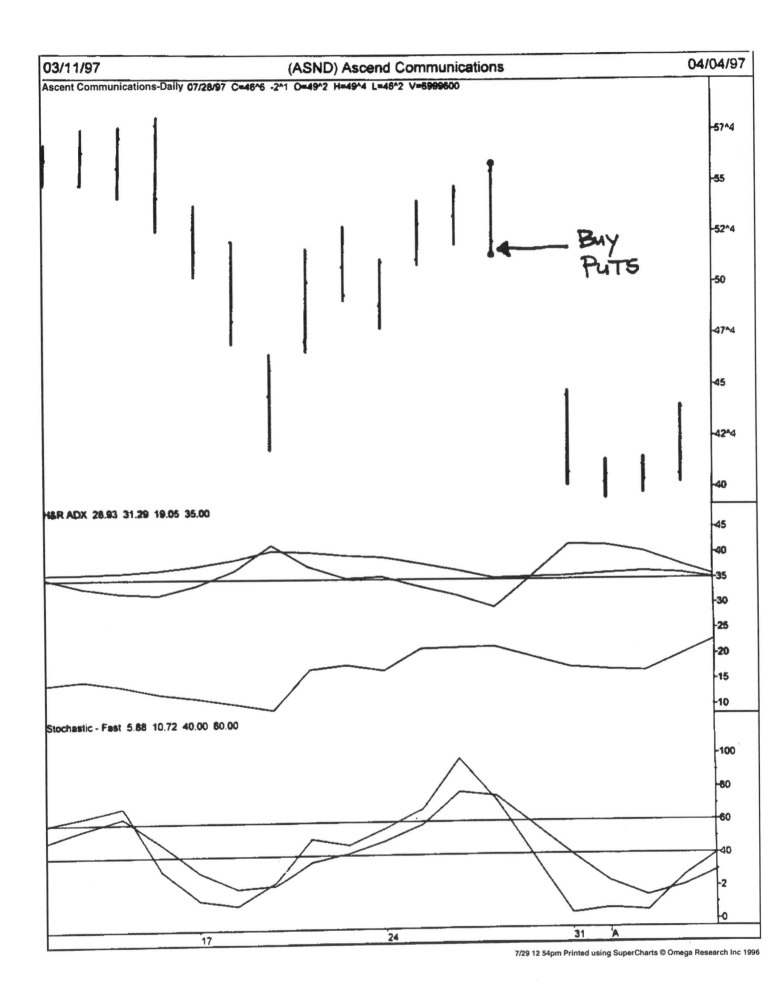

Ascent Communications-Daily 07/28/97 C=46^6 -2^1 O=49^2 H=49^4 L=46^2 V=6999600

H&R ADX 28.93 31.29 19.05 35.00

Stochastic - Fast 5.88 10.72 40.00 60.00

BUY PUTS

Ascend Communications

1. A setup and a trigger to buy the August 60 puts at 8 1/4. The next day, the stock collapses and the puts more than double, closing at 19 1/4.

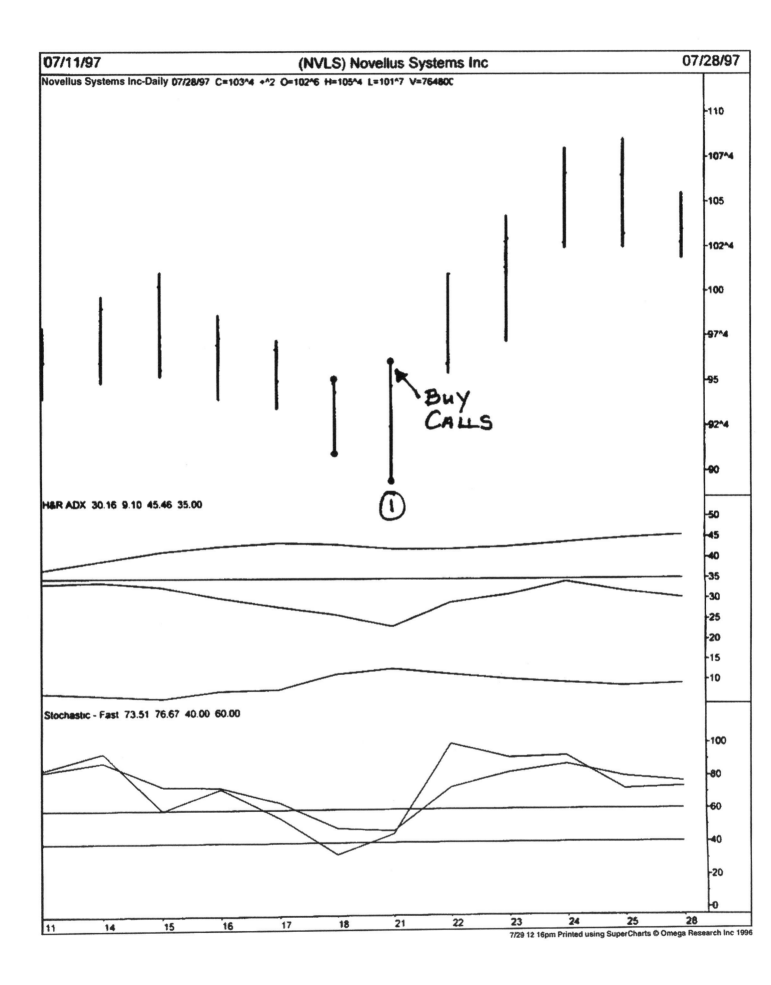

Novellus Systems

1. On July 21, 1997, Novellus has a 5 Day Momentum Method setup. The entry price is above 95 and therefore we will buy the August 90 calls, which are trading at 9.

The stock explodes higher and a few days later our calls close at 17 1/2 for a better than 90 percent gain. (Please remember you would sell your calls beforehand, anytime the stock traded under the July 20 low).

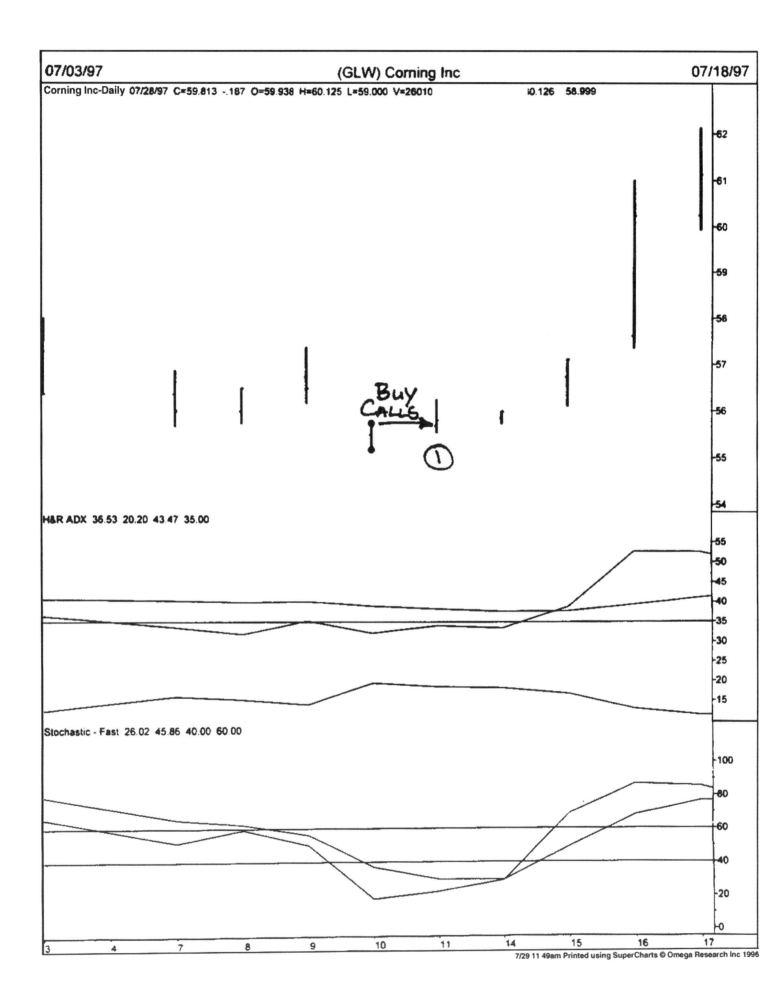

Corning Inc.

1.   A buy setup. We purchase the August 50 calls for 7. Four days later the calls are trading better than 70 percent higher.

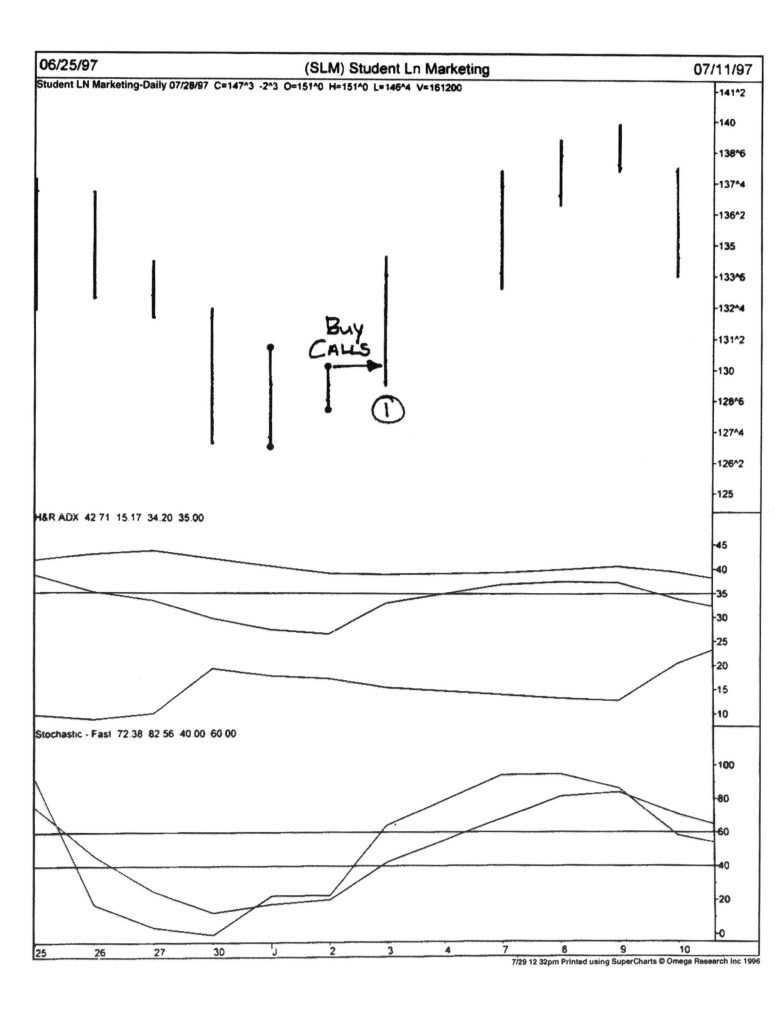

Student Loan Marketing

1.   Another buy setup. The stock is trading a bit above 130, and we purchase the 125 calls at 7 3/4. As you can see, we double our money within 3 days.

In conclusion, I prefer to trade the underlying stocks with all my strategies instead of the options. This is a personal choice and it has worked well for me. If, though, you can overcome the lack of liquidity and large spreads associated with options, they certainly do provide you with a lower cost, higher leveraged means to play the game.

Summary

In conclusion, you will only be trading strongly trending stocks that briefly move opposite the trend and then resume their overall trend. Again, this concept has been successfuly used for decades and in my opinion *The 5 Day Momentum Method* does an excellent job of idenifying and trading this natural tendency.

Remember, this method is correct a little less than half the time. Do not become discouraged. The losses should be small and a handful of gains will be large. This is quite normal for this strategy.

Please re-read this manual and before applying the rules, and paper trade it. It will only make you more confident of both the method and your abilities.

Finally, use good (and disciplined) money management strategies as described previously. This will be the ultimate reason for your success.

Best of Luck,

Jeff Cooper

How to Increase the Potential of *The 5 Day Momentum Method*

The most direct way to participate in large moves is to trade volatile NASDAQ stocks. These are the stocks that move up or down 3–5 points some days. Names like Intel, Microsoft, Dell Computer, and Applied Materials are just a few of the companies that do that. By focusing on these types of stocks, you will be in the position to participate in substantial moves. The drawback though is that by trading these highly volatile names, your risk will be exponentially higher. This means you must put up with the fact that you will be stopped out at a higher rate than less volatile stocks. Please remember this before you trade these (and their counterpart) companies.

Scanning for Setups

It is an inefficient use of time to calculate this strategy by hand. If you use Omega TradeStation or Omega SuperCharts (800-422-8587) you can order the software that will do this for you (please see the end pages of this book). We also offer an add-on module for Equis MetaStock (800-882-3040) users. Although I do not offer an add-on module for Trading Expert by AIQ (800-332-2999), it is another software program that contains all of the necessary indicators (stochastics and ADX) to help you scan for the conditions for a *5 Day Momentum Method* setup on a daily basis. You can also find ADX and +DI/–DI readings on WWW.TRADEHARD.COM. If you have other software, call a programmer or technical support at those organizations. They should be able to create the necessary indicators for you.

Upticks

One of the problems with shorting stocks is the need for an uptick. Stocks can, and sometimes do, drop *points* before upticking. Therefore, to assure this not happening, I recommend you place a sell short stop limit order and give the broker 3/8 or 1/2 point discretion. This means if you wish to sell a stock short the order should read: "sell short at 62 stop limit with 1/2 point discretion." This will assure you that your fill will not be worse than 61 1/2. Remember though that this does not guarantee a fill. You will only get filled if there is an uptick from 61 1/2 to 62 and you are in line and entitled to the fill.

Brokers

You must use a deep discount broker for this strategy. It is critical to your success and the methodology's success to keep transactional costs to an absolute minimum. Read Investors Business Daily and/or Barrons. Both papers have numerous ads from discount brokerage firms who are aggressively competing for your business. Before opening an account make sure they understand what you are accomplishing and also make sure they have the ability to tell you within minutes whether or not you can borrow a stock to short.

ADX AND STOCHASTIC FORMULAS

ADX and +DI/–DI

To determine ADX you must first determine the Directional Movement (DM) readings of a stock or commodity for each day of a 14 day period. Directional Movements are defined below:

+DM (Positive Directional Mvmnt) = High Price (today) – High Price (yesterday)

–DM (Negative Directional Mvmnt) = Low Price (yesterday) – Low Price (today)

Inside days, or days on which today's high or low does not exceed yesterday's high or low, respectively, are counted as 0 for both +DM and –DM.

For each day, if –DM > +DM, +DM = 0. If +DM > –DM, –DM = 0.

You must then determine the True Range for each day for the same 14 day period. True Range (Trnge) is determined by the largest absolute value of:

1. Today's high – today's low, or

2. Today's high – yesterday's close, or

3. Today's low – yesterday's close.

The first +DI and −DI (Directional Indicators) are calculated by summing the Directional Movements for the last 14 days [+DM (14) and −DM (14)] and dividing that by the sum of the True Range for the last 14 days [Trnge (14)]. Please note that the "+" and "−" signs associated with the DM and DI notations are used as a naming convention only and should not be used to alter the values for each factor in the formulas below.

The +DI (14) measures upward movement and the −DI (14) measures downward movement.

+DI (14) = (+DM(14)/trnge(14)) * 100.

−DI (14) = (−DM(14)/trnge(14)) * 100.

To determine the +DM (14) and −DM (14) for the next day:

+DM (14 today) = +DM (14 from previous period) − (+DM (14 from previous period)/14) + +DM (1)

−DM (14 today) = −DM (14 from previous point) − (−DM (14 from previous point)/14) + −DM (1)

Trnge (14) = Trnge (14 from previous point) − (trnge (14 from previous point)/14) + trnge (1)

Then you can proceed to calculate the +DI and −DI as normal:

+DI (14) = (+DM(14)/trnge(14)) * 100.

−DI (14) = (−DM(14)/trnge(14)) * 100.

The DX is the directional movement index. It is calculated by dividing the absolute value of the difference of DIs by the sum of DIs and normalizing this by multiplying by 100. The higher the DX, the more directional the movement; the lower the DX, the less directional the movement. Whether the price movement is up or down is irrelevant to the DX; the DX solely measures how much up or down the movement is (the amount of the movement).

DX = (| (+DI) – (–DI)| / (+DI) + (–DI)) * 100.0

The ADX, Average Directional Movement Index, is a kind of moving average of the DX. Please note that you will need at least 15 days worth of data to first determine the initial readings for the +DM (14), –DM (14), and Trnge (14), and then another 14 days worth of data to calculate the Average DX (ADX) reading.

ADX = (Sum of the DX for the last 14 days)/14

Today's ADX = {(Previous ADX * (14 days – 1)) + Today's DX} / 14 days

According to Jeff Cooper, an ADX value above 30 is considered to be a strongly trending market.

The ADX Formula was created by J. Welles Wilder and is explained comprehensively in his book, *New Concepts in Technical Trading Systems* (ISBN 0-89459-027-8, $65).

You can also obtain ADX readings for the most actively traded stocks from the Stock Traders section of WWW.TRADEHARD.COM, The Ultimate Super-site for Traders.

Stochastic Formula

%K: An unsmoothed Relative Strength Indicator of daily close (Default: 8 days).

%K = ((Current Closing Price – Low Price for the last 8 trading days) / (High Price for the last 8 trading days – Low Price for the last 8 trading days)) * 100

Find Your Own *5 Day Momentum Method* Setups Within Minutes Every Night for the Next Trading Day!

<u>ADD-ON SCANNING SOFTWARE</u>

The *5 Day Momentum Method* System and Indicators for Omega TradeStation and SuperCharts

We have created an add-on module that allows you to identify the setups from The 5 Day Momentum Method on your version of Omega TradeStation and SuperCharts. This software alerts you to daily and intraday signals, plots the setup and also prvides you with a daily printout of each day's entry point. Works with versions 4.0 through 2000i.

Price — $75.

The 5 Day Momentum Method System and Indicators for Equis Metastock

We have created an add-on module that allows you to identify the setups from The 5 Day Momentum Method on your version of Equis MetaStock. This software alerts you to daily signals and also provides you with a daily print-out of each day's entry point. Works with MetaStock versions 6.5 through Professional

Price — $75.

To order with Mastercard, Visa, or American Express call

1-888-794-5400

or send check or money order to:

M. Gordon Publishing Group
445 S. Figueroa St. Suite 2930
Los Angeles, CA 90071

fax: 213-955-4242

RECEIVE JEFF'S BEST 1–3 SETUPS NIGHTLY VIA FAX OR E-MAIL

THE 5 DAY MOMENTUM METHOD
DAILY TRADING SERVICE
— For short-term (3 to 7 days) traders!

Trade the Best 5 Day Momentum Method Setups Everyday!

One of the world's top equity traders shares his daily signals with you. Since Jeff Cooper made his *5 Day Momentum Method Daily Trading Service* available to traders two years ago, the results have been terrific. Over this period, fax subscribers have participated in some of the biggest point gainers on Wall Street.

For Example:

- Recently, subscribers entered St. Joe Corp (SJP) at 96 3/4. Two days later, the stock closed 18 1/4 points higher.
- Subscribers bought Schlumberger (SLB) and National-Oilwell (NOI). Both stocks were exited within a few days for a combined profit of over nine points.
- Jeff's subscribers bought Atwood Oceanics (ATW) at 113 3/4. Three days later, the stock traded more than eight points higher.

The 5 Day Momentum Method Daily Trading Service Works in Both Up Markets and Down Markets

Too many traders lose money when the market drops. *The 5 Day Momentum Method* is structured to not only take advantage of uptrending stocks but also to profit from downtrending stocks. This assures you of participating in both rising markets and declining markets!

For Example:

- Recently, subscribers shorted Merck (MRK) at 90 ½. The next morning they covered at 82, for an 8 ½ point profit.

What You Will Receive Each Evening as a Subscriber

The *5 Day Momentum Method Daily Trading Service* is simple to use. Each evening (5 nights/week) you will receive via your choice of fax or email, Jeff's 1 – 3 best setups for the upcoming day.

His recommendations include:

- The exact entry price
- Whether to buy or sell short
- Where to place your protective stop
- Where to take profits on half your position and on the fifth day where to exit your remaining position.

Price: 1 month – $175 • 3 months – $450 • 6 months – $750 • 1 year – $1,250*

Includes a copy of Jeff's audio tape Trading the Stock Market for a Living.

Other Books from M. GORDON PUBLISHING GROUP

DAVE LANDRY ON SWING TRADING:
A Momentum-Based Approach to Capturing Short-Term Market Moves

DAVE LANDRY

220 Pages   Hardcover $100.00

No time to daytrade? Intermediate-term and long-term trading not enough? Then swing trading is for you. Now David Landry, Director of Trading Research for TradingMarkets.com has put his entire swing trading methodology into one book to teach you how to trade successfully every day.

Dave Landry on Swing Trading takes you from his daily routine to the exact methods David Landry uses day-in and day-out in his own analysis and trading through more than a dozen momentum-based strategies that pinpoint opportunities based on pullbacks and capitalize on false market moves. He also teaches you how to use volatility to select the right stocks and low-risk/high-reward setups. This is a complete manual on swing trading which includes everything the beginner and intermediate trader needs to get started trading quickly.

Dave Landry helps you improve your trading results by exploring and explaining:

- **Trend Qualifiers**—Learn how to precisely identify strongly trending stocks.

- **Stock Selection**—Landry will show you how to narrow down your universe to pick the right stocks to trade.

- **Swing-Trading Strategies**—More than a dozen strategies presented in an easy-to-read, easy-to-understand format, providing you with the specific rules for entry and exit to start identifying the best trading opportunities immediately.

Landry also goes into great detail covering:
   Trading Master Section
   Stock Market Timing
   Money Management
   Trader's Psychology

Finish off your swing-trading education with Landry's thoughts on the winning trading methodology, and so much more!

THE REAL HOLY GRAIL
Money Management Techniques of Top Traders

EDDIE KWONG, EDITOR-IN-CHIEF, TRADINGMARKETS.COM

160 Pages   Soft Cover $45.00

Have you ever had a stock up 10 points, only to have it turn into a loss in a blink of an eye?

The key to attaining success as a trader is: *minimize your losses.* In this book you will receive detailed Money Management lessons from the combined wisdom of **Jeff Cooper, Mark Boucher, Dave Landry, Kevin Haggerty,** and many more experts.

This collection of secrets from the world's Top Traders will teach you: how to use different types of orders to get the best possible price and execution, how to place and trail stops, how to manage positions, how to scale in their position, how to adjust position size relative to account size, how to properly use leverage, how to have the discipline to do the right thing, and more.

The strategies and techniques assembled in this book will give you the tools and insight needed to make better trading decisions, ultimately becoming a smarter trader. **This book is a must for anyone who has the drive to be successful where others have failed.**

STREET SMARTS
High Probability Short-Term Trading Strategies
LAURENCE A. CONNORS
AND LINDA BRADFORD RASCHKE
245 Pages   Hard Cover $175.00

★ ★ ★ ★ (out of 4 stars) . . . Excellent!
Commodity Traders Consumer Report

Published in 1996 and written by Larry Connors and New Market Wizard Linda Raschke, this 245-page manual is considered by many to be one of the best books written on trading futures. Twenty-five years of combined trading experience is divulged as you will learn 20 of their best strategies. Among the methods you will be taught are:

- **Swing Trading**—The backbone of Linda's success. Not only will you learn exactly how to swing trade, you will also learn specific advanced techniques never before made public.

- **News**—Among the strategies revealed is an intraday news strategy they use to exploit the herd when the 8:30 A.M. economic reports are released. This strategy will be especially appreciated by bond traders and currency traders.

- **Pattern Recognition**—You will learn some of the best short-term setup patterns available. Larry and Linda will also teach you how they combine these patterns with other strategies to identify explosive moves.

- **ADX**—In our opinion, ADX is one of the most powerful and misunderstood indicators available to traders. Now, for the first time, they reveal a handful of short-term trading strategies they use in conjunction with this terrific indicator.

- **Volatility**—You will learn how to identify markets that are about to explode and how to trade these exciting situations.

- Also, included are chapters on trading the smart money index, trading Crabel, trading gap reversals, a special chapter on professional money management, and many other trading strategies!

THE BEST OF THE PROFESSIONAL TRADERS JOURNAL SERIES
FROM LARRY CONNORS

Market Timing
42 Pages   Soft Cover $39.95

Learn how to determine which way the Dow, S&Ps, and Nasdaq are going the next day. Professional traders often use sophisticated tools and indicators to help them determine market bias for the next day. Larry Connors gives you his best strategies for determining market direction for the next day in an easy-to-understand and easy-to-use format. Learn how Larry exploits the VIX and TRIN indicators to successfully trade the markets. Backtesting results on just one of the strategies contained in this book has yielded a 288 percent return in just four years!

Includes the Connors VIX Reversal I–V, TRIN Reversals, TRIN Thrusts, and Percent Advance/Decline Indicator (PADI).

TO ORDER CALL: 1-800-797-2584 or 1-213-955-5777 (outside the U.S.)
OR FAX YOUR ORDER TO: 1-213-955-4242
OR MAIL YOUR ORDER TO: M. Gordon Publishing Group, 445 S. Figueroa Street, Suite 2930, Los Angeles, CA 90071
www.mgordonpub.com
All orders please add $6 + $1 each add'l item; Priority Mail: $8 + $1 each add'l item; Airborne Int'l: $25 for shipping and handling.
California residents include 8% sales tax.

Options Trading and Volatility Trading
55 Pages   Soft Cover $39.95

Ninety-seven percent of options traders lose money. Professional trader Larry Connors shares his best options trading strategies with you to help you avoid being just another losing trader. By exploiting stock splits and pricing inefficiencies as well as applying his own strategy, the Connors VIX Reversal, Larry delivers four powerful options methodologies that move the odds decidedly in your favor. In addition, Larry also provides you with the latest research on the little-known, but powerful indicator, historical volatility. From concept to action, Larry explains to you step-by-step how to best use historical volatility to conquer the futures, stock, and options markets.

Includes Trading Volatility with Options, Trading Options with the Connors VIX Reversal, Options on Stock Splits, and Exploiting Over-Priced Stock Sector Options.

Day Trading
44 Pages   Soft Cover $39.95

Everyone who wants to trade professionally must have this book. In it, Larry Connors shares five strategies that will help you become a top-notch day trader. These strategies represent the culmination of over 15 years of trading experience. Larry shows you how to use the powerful ADX indicator to become a winner in the stock market and in the S&Ps. Jeff Cooper also contributes his time-proven Torpedoes strategy to exploit the stock market on an intraday basis. Find out how real traders read the markets during the day.

Includes the 15-Minute ADX Breakout Method, Trading the 15-Minute ADX Breakout Method with Equities, S&P Momentum Day Trading System, Front Running the S&P's, and Torpedoes.

Best Trading Patterns, Volume I
41 Pages   Soft Cover $39.95

Trading is a war and only those traders who are properly prepared will succeed in battle. In *Best Trading Patterns, Volume I*, Larry Connors provides you with an arsenal of short-term trading patterns to successfully trade both stocks and futures. Larry takes you step-by-step through each strategy in this book and defines for you exact entry and protective stop points. If you trade based on gaps, volume, or pullbacks, this book contains the strategies that teach you to successfully trade them all!

Includes The Crash, Burn, and Profit Trading Strategy, Double-Volume Market Top Method, Bottom Reversals, Large-Range Days, Momentum Gaps, Triple-Day Pullbacks, and Turtle Thrusts.

Best Trading Patterns, Volume II
58 Pages   Soft Cover $39.95

If you can't get enough of Larry Connors' time-tested, market-proven, short-term (three- to seven-day holding periods) trading strategies, this is the book for you. Successful trader and hedge fund manager Larry Connors gives you seven potent technical trading strategies to conquer the stock and futures markets. Unlike other trading books that talk *around* trading, Connors' *Best Trading Patterns, Volume II* gives you exact rules for entry along with several illustrated examples to show you how these strategies have traded in the past. This book is designed to get you from reading to trading immediately.

Includes the Spent Market Trading Pattern, 1-2-3-4s, The 8-Day High/Low Reversal Method, 10% Oops, Momentum Moving Averages, Gipsons, and Wide-Range Exhaustion Gap Reversals.

HIT AND RUN TRADING
The Short-Term Stock Traders' Bible
JEFF COOPER
160 Pages   Hard Cover $100.00

Written by professional equities trader Jeff Cooper, this best-selling manual teaches traders how to day-trade and short-term trade stocks. Jeff's strategies identify daily the ideal stocks to trade and point out the exact entry and protective exit point. Most trades risk 1 point or less and last from a few hours to a few days.

Among the strategies taught are:

- **Stepping In Front Of Size**—You will be taught how to identify when a large institution is desperately attempting to buy or sell a large block of stock. You will then be taught how to step in front of this institution before the stock explodes or implodes. This strategy many times leads to gains from 1/4 point to 4 points within minutes.

- **1-2-3-4s**—Rapidly moving stocks tend to pause for a few days before they explode again. You will be taught the three-day setup that consistently triggers solid gains within days.

- **Expansion Breakouts**—Most breakouts are false! You will learn the one breakout pattern that consistently leads to further gains. This pattern alone is worth the price of the manual.

- Also, you will learn how to trade market explosions (Boomers), how to trade secondary offerings, how to trade Slingshots, and you will learn a number of other profitable strategies that will make you a stronger trader.

HIT AND RUN TRADING II
Capturing Explosive Short-Term Moves in Stocks
JEFF COOPER
212 Pages   Hard Cover $100.00

212 fact-filled pages of new trading strategies from Jeff Cooper. You will learn the best momentum continuation and reversal strategies to trade. You will also be taught the best day-trading strategies that have allowed Jeff to make his living trading for the past decade. Also included is a special five-chapter bonus section entitled, "Techniques of a Professional Trader" where Jeff teaches you the most important aspects of trading, including money management, stop placement, daily preparation, and profit-taking strategies.

If you aspire to become a full-time professional trader, this is the book for you.

Hit and Run Lessons: Mastering the Trading Strategies
JEFF COOPER
175 Pages   Hard Cover $75.00

Do you ever wish you could spend a few weeks looking over Jeff Cooper's shoulders watching him trade? If so, then *Hit and Run Lessons: Mastering the Trading Strategies* is for you. In it, Jeff Cooper draws from his Daily Learning Sheets and gives you a blow-by-blow analysis of the actual trading setups that he has been trading for the past four years. You'll not only see what Jeff does, but also learn how Jeff thinks when he stalks trading opportunities through Pullbacks, Breakouts, Reversals, Stepping-In-Front-Of-Size, and more.

This book is a must for every trader's collection.

SOFTWARE

ABOUT THE AUTHOR

Jeff Cooper is a full-time, professional equities trader. A graduate of New York University, he is also the author of *Hit and Run Trading I* (1996), *Hit and Run Trading II* (1998), and *Hit and Run Lessons: Mastering the Trading Strategies* (1999). You can read what Jeff has to say about the market daily at 9:30 A.M. EST at www.TradingMarkets.com.

FREE REPORT

Maximize Your Trading Profits Immediately

David Landry, TradingMarkets.com Director of Research, has put together a set of simple money management rules to help all traders become more successful in his report *The True Secret to Trading Success: Simple Money Management Rules That Will Make You a More Profitable Trader!*

To obtain this report, send your request along with your name and address to:

M. Gordon Publishing Group, Inc.
Department 5D
445 S. Figueroa Street, Suite 2930
Los Angeles, CA 90071

Or

Fax your information to 213-955-4242.

Your report will be mailed immediately.